Networks Social Studies

Our Community and Beyond

Saving Money

PunchStock/Getty Images

Gulf of Mexico

C. McIntyre/PhotoLink/Getty Images

Following Rules

Rich Reid/National Geographic/Getty Images

History Museum

Draw a picture of an artifact from long ago.

Mc
Graw
Hill
Education

Send all inquiries to:
McGraw-Hill Education
8787 Orion Place
Columbus, OH 43240

ISBN: 978-0-02-146204-9
MHID: 0-02-146204-6

Printed in the United States of America.

5 6 7 8 9 QLM 22 21 20 19 18 17

PROGRAM AUTHORS

James A. Banks, Ph.D.
Kerry and Linda Killinger Endowed Chair
 in Diversity Studies and Director, Center
 for Multicultural Education
University of Washington
Seattle, Washington

Kevin P. Colleary, Ed.D.
Curriculum and Teaching Department
Graduate School of Education
Fordham University
New York, New York

Linda Greenow, Ph.D.
Associate Professor and Chair
Department of Geography
State University of New York at New Paltz
New Paltz, New York

Walter C. Parker, Ph.D.
Professor of Social Studies Education,
 Adjunct Professor of Political Science
University of Washington
Seattle, Washington

Emily M. Schell, Ed.D.
Visiting Professor, Teacher Education
San Diego State University
San Diego, California

Dinah Zike
Educational Consultant
Dinah-Might Adventures, L.P.
San Antonio, Texas

CONTRIBUTING AUTHORS

James M. Denham, Ph.D.
Professor of History and Director,
 Lawton M. Chiles, Jr., Center for
 Florida History
Florida Southern College
Lakeland, Florida

M.C. Bob Leonard, Ph.D.
Professor, Hillsborough Community
 College
Director, Florida History Internet Center
Ybor City, Florida

Jay McTighe
Educational Author and Consultant
McTighe and Associates Consulting
Columbia, Maryland

Timothy Shanahan, Ph.D.
Professor of Urban Education &
 Director, Center for Literacy
College of Education
University of Illinois at Chicago

ACADEMIC CONSULTANTS

Tom Daccord
Educational Technology Specialist
Co-Director, EdTechTeacher
Boston, Massachusetts

Joe Follman
Service Learning Specialist
Director, Florida Learn & Serve

Cathryn Berger Kaye, M.A.
Service Learning Specialist
Author, *The Complete Guide to Service
 Learning*

Justin Reich
Educational Technology Specialist
Co-Director, EdTechTeacher
Boston, Massachusetts

My Book

My Computer

networks

Go online and
find a video about
American holidays.

My Cover

Use your cover to help
you solve this riddle:
*I lived a long time ago.
I was the first President
of the United States.
Who am I?*

Explore! UNIT 2 Where We Live

BIG IDEA Location affects how people live.

My Book

My Computer

networks

Go online and find this neighborhood map.

My Cover

On your cover, find someone looking at a map. Where do you think he is going?

_____

Keep going!
Next, we'll explore economics!

v

Explore! UNIT 3 Beginning Economics

BIG IDEA Economics affects choices.

My Book

My Computer

networks

 Go online and find a video about goods and services.

My Cover

Find the toy store on your cover. What are some things you would buy at this store? Draw a picture here.

©MBI/Alamy

vi

Explore! UNIT 4 Good Citizens

BIG IDEA People's actions affect others.

My Book

My Computer

networks

 Go online and find a video about rules in a community.

My Cover

Find four American symbols on your cover. Once you spot them, write their names on the lines below.

_____

_____

_____

_____

Keep going!
Next, we'll explore skills and maps.

Explore! Skills and Maps

Skills

Reading Skills

Primary Sources

My Computer

networks

 Go online to learn more about pictures from long ago.

National Archives and Records Administration

My Cover

Find the museum on your cover. Draw a picture of something you might find at the museum about life long ago.

Explore! Skills and Maps

Maps

My Cover

Find a large lake. Write it here.

_____

My Computer

networks

Go online to explore this interactive map.

Reference Section

People and Traditions

BIG IDEA People and events shape history.

History is the story of people and events from other times and places. Many of the stories in this unit tell about important people and events. You may already know about some of them. Others may be new to you. As you read, think about what these people and events mean to you.

Show As You Go!

After you read each lesson in this unit, complete these activities to practice what you are learning!

Lesson 1

After you read Lesson 1:

○ Draw or paste a picture of a special place in your community.

Our Community Museum

Lesson 1

Lesson 2

Lesson 2

After you read Lesson 2:

○ Draw or paste a picture to show how your community celebrates Independence Day.

Lesson 3

After you read Lesson 3:

○ Draw or paste a picture of a leader in your community.

Lesson 4

After you read Lesson 4:

○ Write one or two sentences that tell why your community is special.

Lesson 3

Lesson 4

Reading Skill

Common Core Standards
RI.9: Identify basic similarities in and differences between two texts on the same topic.

Finding Similarities and Differences

When you read, think about how things are similar or different. Things that are similar are the same in some ways. Things that are different are not the same.

Learn It

To find similarities and differences:

1. **Read the stories and look at the pictures.**

2. **Ask yourself how they are the same.**

3. **Ask how they are different.**

Hi! My name is Sarah. I have chores at home. Before I go to school, I milk the cows and feed the chickens.

Hi! My name is Ava. I have chores, too! On Saturdays, I clean my room and help take out the trash.

Same

Different

Write the similarities and differences from the story on page 4 in the chart below. Write what is different between Sarah and Ava in the outer circles. Write what is the same in the middle.

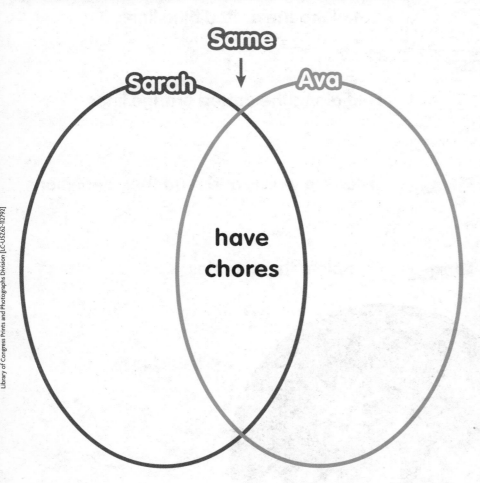

Same

Sarah

Ava

have chores

Read the paragraphs below. (Circle) the similarities. Underline the differences.

Long ago, children went to school in one-room schoolhouses. Children of all ages learned together.

Today, most children go to school in big buildings. Most of the time, each class has its own room.

Words to Know

FOLDABLES®

The list below shows some important words you will learn in this unit. Their definitions can be found on the next page. Read the words.

history

fact

holiday

culture

character

fiction

The Foldable on the next page will help you learn these important words. Follow the steps below to make your Foldable.

Step 1  Cut along the dotted blue lines.

Step 2 Fold along the dotted orange lines.

Step 3 Trace the words and read their definitions.

Step 4 Complete the activities.

Can you name this important person? Write his name on the line below.

_____

Cut Here
Cut Here

Fold Here

Circle the fact below.

1. Polar bears are tiny.
2. Farmers grow oranges.
3. It is always rainy in Alaska.

What is your favorite holiday? Write about it below.

_____

_____

History is the story of people and events from other times and places.

A **fact** is something that is true and not made up.

A **holiday** is a day when we remember and honor a special event or person.

Do not fold

Do not fold

Do not fold

Do not fold

Culture is the way a group of people live. It is made up of their special food, music, and art.

Fold Here

Character is used to describe someone who is honest, brave, or responsible.

Fiction is something that is not true.

Many people eat foods from different cultures. Write about a special food you eat.

_____

Draw a picture of someone who shows good character.

Write another example of fiction on the blank line.

People can fly like birds.
Money grows on trees.

_____

Cut Here

Cut Here

Cut Here

holiday

fact

history

Fold Here

Fold Here

nutrition

character

culture

Primary sources are written or made by someone who saw an event happen. They teach us about people, places, and events.

An **artifact** is a primary source. Artifacts are objects that were made or used by people from the past, or long ago. Artifacts can tell us how people lived at that time.

These stone spear points are artifacts. Early hunters used tools like these when hunting.

 Document-Based Questions

1. Look at the artifacts on this page. What do they show?

_____

_____

networks
There's More Online!
● Skill Builders
● Resource Library

2. How were these artifacts used?

_____

_____

Change Over Time

Lesson 1

(?) Essential Question

How has life changed over time?

What do you think?

_____

_____

_____

_____

_____

Word Hunt

Find and circle these words:

history	*fact
time line	community
technology	

Find one new word.

_____

(l)John Flournoy/McGraw-Hill Education, (c)Courtesy of the State Archives of Florida, (cr)Library of Congress - Prints and Photographs Division [LC-USZC4-11368], (r)Library of Congress Prints and Photographs Division [LC-USZC4-4961]

What Is History?

History tells the story of people and events from other times and places. You may already know about people and events from the past, or long ago. Look at these pictures. The people and events on these pages are all a part of history.

Circle the ones you already know about.

10

Library of Congress Prints and Photographs Division [LC-USZ62-7816]

There are many ways you can learn about history. You can ask your parents and grandparents about life long ago. You can visit a museum or read a book about people and events. You can also use primary sources like pictures, letters, and artifacts.

When you read about history, look for historical **facts**. A fact is something that is true and not made up.

1. **One of the sentences below is a fact. The other is not. Circle the one that is a fact.**

   a. **You are in first grade.**

   b. **All grades are in the same classroom.**

2. **Write one more fact about school.**

_____

_____

_____

Family Life Then

Long ago, families lived in one-room cabins without electricity or running water. They used candles and oil lamps to see in the dark. They cooked their meals over an open fire.

Children had chores like they do today. Most of the time, children would do their chores before and after school. For many children, that meant helping out on the farm.

For fun, girls played games like hopscotch. They also played with cornhusk dolls. Boys played with jacks or marbles.

Underline four facts that describe family life in the past.

Oleksiy Maksymenko/Alamy Images

Family Life Now

Today, our homes have electricity and running water. We cook meals in ovens and store food in refrigerators.

Children still do many of the same things they did long ago. They go to school and play games. They also have chores. But today, some children get money for doing their chores.

Children still play games today. Games are much different from long ago. Today, children play video or computer games.

Draw a picture of your home.

Media Center

Use the Internet and other sources to find out:

1. What chores did children do long ago compared to today?

_____

2. What games do children play now that they didn't have in the past?

_____

Use Time Lines

A **time line** shows an order of events. Time lines show what happened first, next, and last. They can show days, weeks, months, or years.

Look at the time line below. It shows events in Jack's life. Read the time line from left to right. Events on the left happened first.

1 year old
I learned to walk.

2 years old
I had a party.

3 years old
I visited my grandparents.

14

The McGraw-Hill Companies

1. What happened when Jack was 2 years old?

_____

_____

2. When did Jack go camping?

_____

_____

Draw a picture to show what happens when Jack is 6 years old.

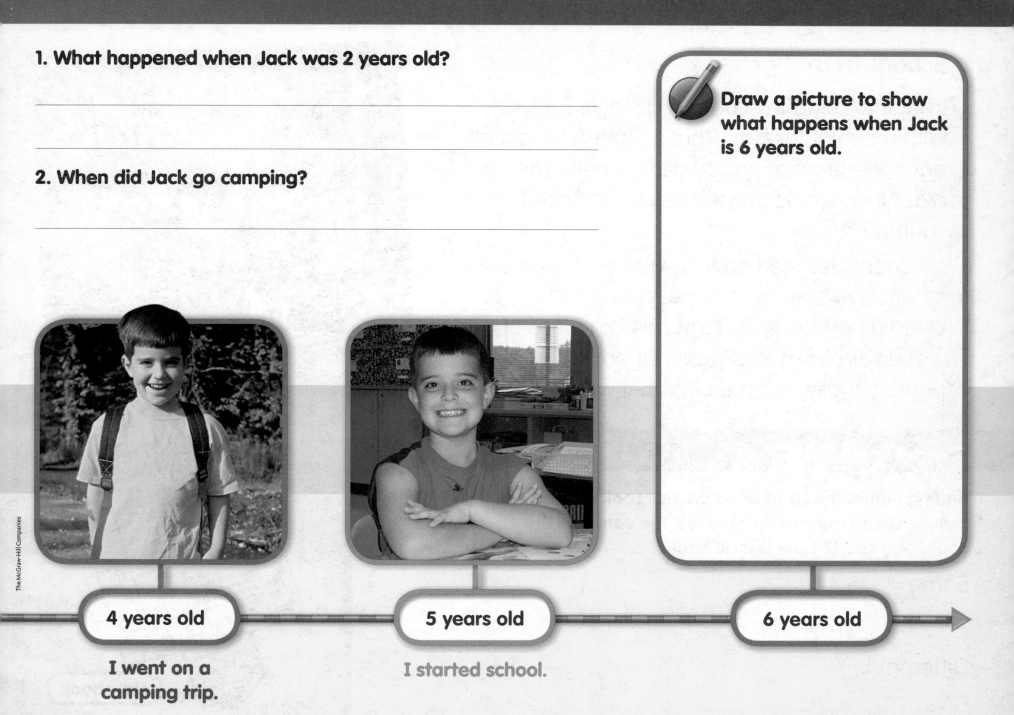

4 years old

I went on a camping trip.

5 years old

I started school.

6 years old

School Then

Imagine going to school in a single room with much older kids. That's right! A long time ago, one teacher taught all students. The older kids would sometimes help teach the younger ones.

Students learned how to write on slates, or small chalkboards. They learned how to read using a hornbook. A hornbook is a piece of wood with a sheet of paper attached to it. The paper usually had the alphabet written on it.

Hornbook

Reading Skill

Finding Similarities and Differences **Look at the picture of the hornbook. How is it the same as the books you read? How is it different?**

Same:

_____

Different:

_____

16

School Now

Today, schools are bigger than they were long ago. Students go to school in buildings with many rooms. Most classes have their own classroom.

Schools have many tools to help students learn. Some classrooms have computers, TVs, and whiteboards. Many schools also have a computer lab and a library.

Draw a picture of your school.

1. What were classrooms like in the past?

_____

_____

2. What are classrooms like today?

_____

_____

17

Community Life Then

You and your family live in a **community**. A community is a place where people live, work, and play. Long ago, most communities were smaller than they are today. There were fewer homes and more open space between them. People would walk or ride horses into town for food, supplies, mail, and fun.

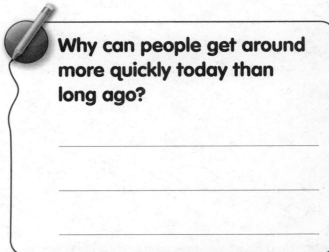

Why can people get around more quickly today than long ago?

_____

_____

_____

Community Life Now

Today, most communities are larger than they were long ago. As more people moved into communities, they built more homes, roads, and buildings.

Today, many communities have schools, libraries, and parks. Some communities also have stores, museums, and hospitals.

Work Then

Work has also changed over time. Long ago, many people worked on farms. As communities grew, more jobs were created. People began to work on railroads, in offices, and in factories. A factory is a place where workers make things that people need and want.

Work Now

Today, very few people work on farms. **Technology** has changed the way we work. Technology is the science of making things faster and easier. Technology allows people to build machines and computers. Machines and computers changed the kind of work people do. Today, many people work in offices using computers and the Internet.

Underline three facts you learned about work then and now.

Not long ago, people in offices did not use computers like they do today. Many computers needed a lot of space. In fact, they needed a room all to themselves! Use the media center to find out how computers have changed over time.

21

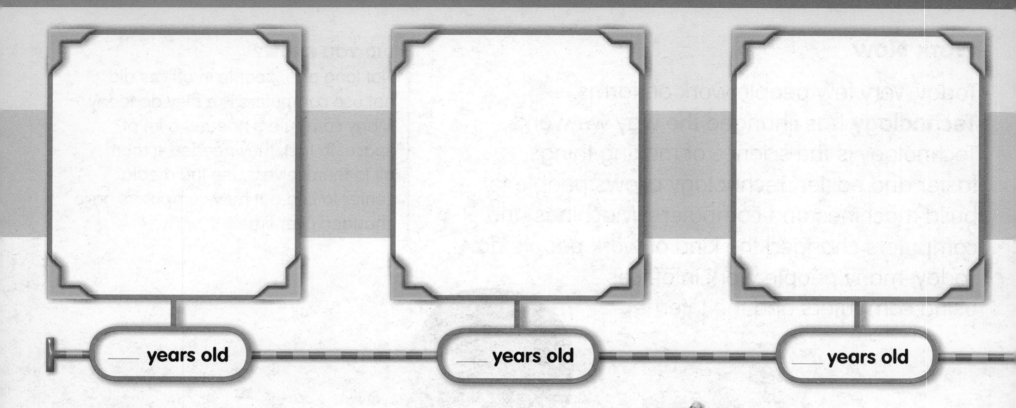

_____ years old   _____ years old   _____ years old

My Life Time Line

You just learned about how life has changed from long ago to today. Now, think about how your life has changed. Have you moved to a new place or a new school? Do you have a new baby brother or sister? Maybe you were student of the month and got good grades on your report card.

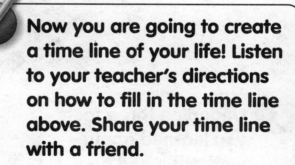

Now you are going to create a time line of your life! Listen to your teacher's directions on how to fill in the time line above. Share your time line with a friend.

Talking and Moving

Transportation links people and places. Moving is easier today than in the past. Cars, buses, and airplanes carry families from place to place.

Communication is the way people share ideas, thoughts, or information. It links people and message between places. Today, letters travel fast on airplanes. E-mail on computers goes around the world in less than a minute.

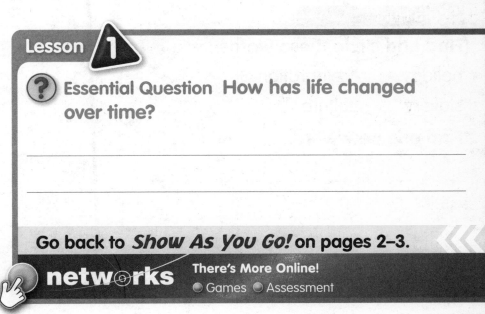

Lesson 1

? **Essential Question** How has life changed over time?

_____

_____

Go back to *Show As You Go!* on pages 2–3.

netw⚙rks **There's More Online!**
● Games ● Assessment

x

23

2 Special Holidays

? Essential Question

Why do we celebrate people and events?

What do you think?

_____

_____

_____

You just learned about life long ago and today. Now you will learn about **holidays**. A holiday is a day when we remember and honor a special event or person.

Word Hunt

Find and circle these words:

holiday   *celebration

slavery   culture

Find one new word.

_____

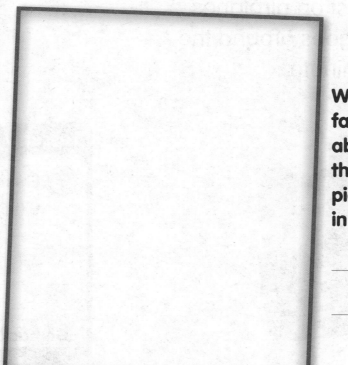

What is a special day your family celebrates? Write about your special day on the lines below. Draw a picture of the celebration in the box to the left.

_____

_____

Let's Celebrate!

During the year, Americans come together to honor and celebrate our nation's people and events. Look at the pictures of the holidays. Draw a ☆ next to your favorite holiday.

May

Cinco de Mayo   Memorial Day

February

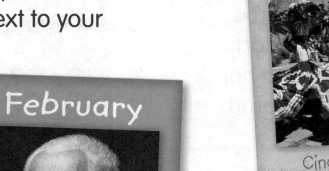

Presidents' Day

January

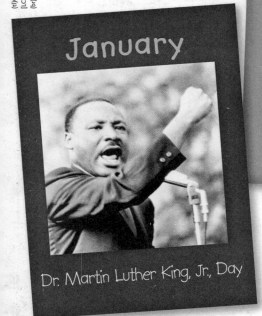

Dr. Martin Luther King, Jr., Day

July

Independence Day

November

Veterans Day   Thanksgiving

Dr. Martin Luther King, Jr., Day

Many years ago some people were treated unfairly because of the color of their skin. Dr. Martin Luther King, Jr., worked hard so that all Americans would be treated the same. Today, we remember and honor Dr. Martin Luther King, Jr., in January. One way to honor him is by working with others in our community.

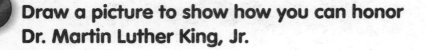

Draw a picture to show how you can honor Dr. Martin Luther King, Jr.

Presidents' Day

In February, we celebrate Presidents' Day. On this day, we remember the birthdays of Presidents George Washington and Abraham Lincoln. Presidents' Day is also a day to celebrate all of our other Presidents.

Happy Birthday George and Abraham!

I helped fight for our country's freedom and became our first President. I am also known as the Father of Our Country.

I was the 16th President. I helped to end **slavery**. Slavery is when one person takes away another person's freedom.

(Circle) one fact you learned about both Presidents.

27

Cinco de Mayo

Cinco de Mayo means the "fifth of May" in Spanish. It celebrates the day that Mexico won a battle against France. Today, many people in the United States celebrate Cinco de Mayo. It is a time to learn about Mexican American **culture**. Culture is the way a group of people live. Culture is made up of a group's special food, music, and art. We can share our culture with one another.

Mexico

Glow Images

Reading Skill

Make Connections Making connections to the text helps us see how things are related. What other holiday celebrates culture?

Memorial Day

We celebrate Memorial Day each May. On this day, we honor and show respect for our soldiers who died in war. Many people celebrate Memorial Day by raising the flag, marching in parades, or having picnics.

Veterans Day

In November, we celebrate Veterans Day. A veteran is someone who protects, or looks after, our country. Veterans Day is our chance to say "thank you" to the brave men and women who protect our country. Many towns and cities have parades in honor of our veterans.

Write a thank you letter to a war veteran.

Dear Soldier,
Thank you for _____

_____

_____

_____

From,

_____

(your name)

Independence Day

A long time ago, America belonged to another country. America's leaders met in 1776 to sign the Declaration of Independence. This important paper said that America wanted to be free.

Thomas Jefferson and Benjamin Franklin were two of these brave leaders. Thanks to them and others, we now celebrate our independence. The Fourth of July is the birthday of our country. It is also called Independence Day.

Many people wave our flag on this day. Do you know what the colors of our flag stand for? The red stands for courage. The white stands for purity, or goodness. The blue stands for loyalty.

Create your own classroom flag to the right. Make sure it has many colors and shapes!

Library of Congress Prints and Photographs Division [LC-USZC2-2711]

Thanksgiving Day

A long time ago, Pilgrims came to live in America. Their lives were very hard. They had trouble growing enough food. A group of Native Americans helped the Pilgrims. They showed the Pilgrims how to grow new crops. The Pilgrims wanted to thank the Native Americans for their help. They invited the Native Americans for a special meal. This day became known as Thanksgiving Day.

DID YOU KNOW?

In 1863, President Abraham Lincoln made Thanksgiving Day a national holiday. We now celebrate Thanksgiving on the last Thursday in November every year.

Lesson 2

? **Essential Question Why do we celebrate people and events?**

_____

_____

_____

Go back to *Show As You Go!* on pages 2–3.

netw⦿rks   There's More Online!
● Games ● Assessment

American Heroes

? **Essential Question**

How do people show character?
What do you think?

_____

_____

_____

_____

Word Hunt

Find and (circle) these words:

character   *honesty

*courage   *responsibility

Find one new word.

_____

In this lesson, you will read stories about Americans who have shown good **character**. Character means showing honesty, courage, or responsibility.

Honest Abe

Abraham Lincoln believed in hard work and **honesty**. As a young man, Abraham helped his father work on their farm. He chopped wood, planted crops, and carried water. Abraham was a good farmer, but he had other dreams.

When Abraham grew up, he left his father's farm. Abraham had many jobs. He worked on a boat moving goods and people. He was a soldier. He ran a post office and worked at a store.

Abraham enjoyed working in the store. One day, Abraham charged a customer too much money. He walked many miles to return the customer's change. From that day on, Abraham was known as "Honest Abe."

Reading Skill

Use Text Features A title helps you understand what you will read. What do the titles "American Heroes" and "Honest Abe" tell you about Abraham Lincoln?

_____

_____

_____

Good morning, Mrs. Appleby. How can I help you?

Good morning, Mr. Lincoln. I'd like flour, wheat, sugar, beans, rice, and tea. Oh, and don't forget the honey this time!

Well, that's the last of it. That'll be $1.35.

Thanks, Mr. Lincoln. I'll be back next month.

Oh no! I charged Mrs. Appleby 3 extra cents. I must do the honest thing and return her change!

President Abraham Lincoln

Abraham believed that our words and actions are very important. He said, "Resolve to be honest at all events."

In 1860, Abraham Lincoln became the 16th President of the United States. At the time, some people in our country wanted to end slavery. Others did not.

Think of a person you have read about who has shown honesty. Write his or her name below.

_____

Focus on Honesty

How did Abraham Lincoln become known as "Honest Abe"?

_____

_____

_____

People on the two sides of our country fought against each other in a war called the Civil War. Abraham worked to keep our country together during the war. When the Civil War ended, slavery ended, too.

Franklin D. Roosevelt

Franklin D. Roosevelt became the 32nd President of the United States in 1933. He is the only President to be elected four times.

Harriet Tubman's Courage

Harriet Tubman was born in Maryland around 1820. She was born into slavery. People in slavery worked long hours with little rest. They could not go to school or make their own choices.

Harriet heard about something called the Underground Railroad. The Underground Railroad was not a train.

Frederick Douglass also helped the Underground Railroad. He had learned to read early in his life and wrote many books on his journey to freedom.

Library of Congress Prints and Photographs Division [LC-US262-7816]

Reading Skill

Make Connections When you make connections, you think about how people, ideas, or events are related. What do Abraham Lincoln and Harriet Tubman have in common?

_____

_____

_____

The Underground Railroad was a group of people who helped others in slavery escape, or run away. The Underground Railroad gave people food and a place to rest until they reached a place that did not have slavery.

In 1849 Harriet ran away to Pennsylvania. She was finally free. Harriet wanted to help others find freedom. This meant she had to risk her own life. Harriet joined the Underground Railroad and helped many people escape slavery. Today, we remember Harriet Tubman for her **courage**.

Focus on Courage

Write about someone you know who has shown courage.

_____

_____

_____

_____

37

Women Leaders

Dorothea Dix and Mary McLeod Bethune were important leaders during the civil rights. Civil rights are the basic rights that all citizens should have. Many African Americans faced discrimination. Discrimination is the unfair treatment of a person or group because of their race, gender, age, or beliefs.

Bethune's view of the world was shaped by what she saw and experienced in the South. She was a leader in the fight for education and equal rights. She received many honors and awards.

Dorothea Dix

Mary McLeod Bethune

She worked for the government under many Presidents. She gave advice about civil rights and equality for all people.

Dorothea Dix also fought for equal rights. She helped the mentally ill receive better care than they were during her time. She was a nurse leader in the Civil War and helped make education more available to young girls.

How did Dorothea Dix and Mary McLeod Bethune help during the civil right?

_____

_____

_____

Focus on Responsibility

How did these leaders show responsibility to their communities?

_____

_____

_____

Lesson 3

? Essential Question **How do people show character?**

_____

_____

_____

Go back to *Show As You Go!* on pages 2–3.

networks   There's More Online!
● Games ● Assessment

Sharing Stories

Why do we read stories?
What do you think?

_____

_____

_____

Word Hunt

Find and (circle) these words:

tall tale   *exaggerate

fable   fiction

nonfiction

Find one new word.

_____

TALL TALES

Have you ever exaggerated? When you **exaggerate**, you make something more important, or bigger than it is. The story on the next page is a **tall tale**. Tall tales exaggerate details in a story.

As you read the tall tale on the next page, <u>underline</u> the details that are exaggerated.

Brand X Pictures/PunchStock

PAUL BUNYAN

A long time ago, there lived a lumberjack named Paul Bunyan. A lumberjack is someone who cuts down trees for a living. Paul became famous for his size and strength. Stories say that he was more than 50 feet tall. Paul was so strong he could cut down a hundred trees with one swing!

41

Paul had a loyal friend named Babe. Babe was a blue ox. Some people say Babe was as big as a mountain. Babe followed Paul wherever he traveled.

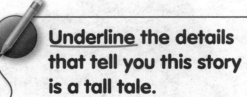

Underline the details that tell you this story is a tall tale.

Reading Skill

Clarify Words and Phrases
Think about the words "loyal friend." What do you think the word "loyal" means? Read the story again to look for clues.

One hot summer day, Paul and Babe cleared an entire forest. Paul wanted to reward Babe with a fountain of water. He began to dig deep holes into the soil, looking for water. Paul dug so deep that the holes became the Great Lakes!

FABLES

Have you ever read a **fable**? A fable is a story that teaches a lesson. Fables often use animals or other things that talk and act like people. As you read this fable, think about who or what talks and acts like a person.

THE WIND AND THE SUN

One day the wind and the sun were fighting over who was stronger. "I can pull out trees by their roots and make homes shake with fear," said Wind.

"I light up the world," said Sun.

Just then, they saw a man walking down a long road. Sun had a thought. "Let's see who can make the man take off his coat. You can go first." Then Sun hid behind a cloud.

What two things are acting like people?

_____

_____

45

Wind blew a strong gust of air, shaking all the trees in the forest. But this didn't stop the man. He frowned at the wind and kept walking.

Then, Wind blew heavier and stronger gusts of air. The man found it very hard to walk, but he held on tight to his coat. After a long while, Wind gave up.

Underline what happened to the man when Wind had his turn.

46

Then, it was Sun's turn. Sun began to shine her rays of light through the forest. Warm rays of light shined through the trees. The animals ran out of their shelters and were happy again. The man started to whistle as he walked. Then, he took off his coat.

What is the moral, or lesson, of the story? Write your answer below.

_____

_____

_____

Reading Skill

Clarify Words and Phrases
(Circle) the clues that help you understand the phrase "rays of light." Then write what you think it means below.

_____

_____

_____

47

Fiction or Nonfiction

The tall tale and fable you just read are **fiction**. Fiction is something that is not true. Not everything you read is fiction! Some stories are **nonfiction**. Nonfiction tells about something that is true. Is the article below fiction or nonfiction?

When I grow up....

Abby lives in sunny California. When Abby grows up, she wants to be a meteorologist. A meteorologist reports the weather. Abby likes sunny days because she can go to the beach. On rainy days, she likes to look for rainbows. The only kind of weather Abby doesn't like is the Santa Ana winds!

With many historical stories, some of what we read is fact and some is fiction. In Lesson 1, you learned that a fact is something that is true and not made up. In this lesson, you read stories that are fiction, or not true.

Read the sentences below. Circle fact or fiction for each sentence.

1. People can be more than 50 feet tall!

   Fact   **Fiction**

2. The sun and the wind can talk.

   Fact   **Fiction**

3. A meteorologist reports the weather.

   Fact   **Fiction**

Fact = true

Fiction = not true

Lesson **4**

? **Essential Question** **Why do we read stories?**

_____

_____

_____

_____

Go back to *Show As You Go!* **on pages 2–3.**

networks   There's More Online!
● Games ● Assessment

49

Use the words in the box to complete the puzzle.

Word Bank

history	character	fiction
community	fact	holiday
time line		

ACROSS

1. something that is not true
3. a day when we remember a special event or person
6. a place where people live, work, and play
7. a line that shows an order of events

DOWN

2. when people show honesty, responsibility, or courage they show this
4. the story of people and events from other times
5. something that is true and not made up

Oleksiy Maksymenko/Alamy Images

Big Idea Project

You are going to create a poster to place in a classroom museum. Read the list below to see what you should include on your poster.

As you work, check off each task as you complete it.

My poster . . .   **Yes it does!**

1. shows information about one of these topics: family life, school, community life, or work. ○

2. shows pictures or artifacts from long ago. ○

3. is colorful and interesting. ○

4. includes sentences describing how life has changed over time. ○

🏠 **HOME LIFE**

This is life long ago. It is different from life today. Long ago, there was a milkman who would leave milk at your door. Some things are still the same. We still watch t.v. and cook our meals.

Think About the Big Idea

BIG IDEA 💡 People and events shape history. In your own words, explain the Big Idea on the lines below.

_____

_____

UNIT 2
Where We Live

BIG IDEA Location affects how people live.

Have you ever used a map to find a new place? Have you ever looked at a globe to see where you live in our big world? In this unit, you will learn about maps and globes. As you read, think about how maps and globes help you learn about where you live.

networks

connected.mcgraw-hill.com
- Skill Builders
- Vocabulary Flashcards

52

Show As You Go!

After you read each lesson in this unit, use the map and the activities on these pages to practice what you are learning!

Lesson **1**

After you read Lesson 1:

◯ Give your map a title.

◯ Label the compass rose with the four cardinal directions.

Lesson **2**

After you read Lesson 2:

◯ Circle the bodies of water that surround Florida.

◯ Look at the symbol for the Florida Keys. Draw this symbol on the map key.

◯ Draw a next to Tallahassee. Draw this symbol for Tallahassee in the map key.

Lesson **3**

After you read Lesson 3:

◯ Draw a picture of a home to show where you live.

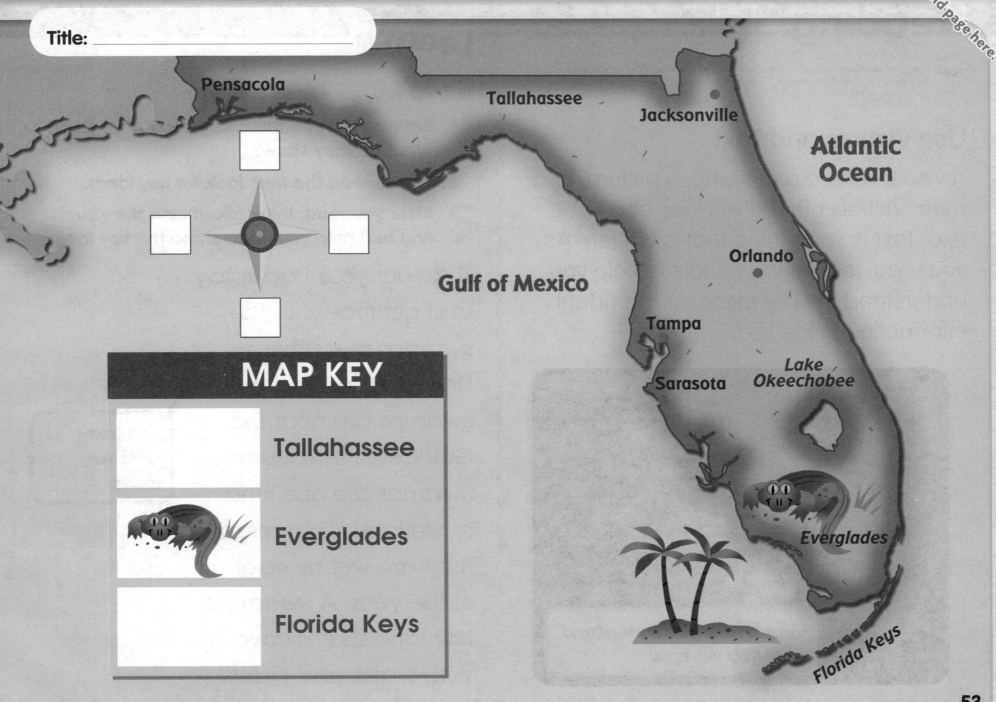

Title: _____

Pensacola

Tallahassee

Jacksonville

Atlantic Ocean

Gulf of Mexico

Orlando

Tampa

Sarasota

Lake Okeechobee

Everglades

Florida Keys

MAP KEY

	Tallahassee
	Everglades
	Florida Keys

Reading Skill

 Common Core Standards
RI.6: Distinguish between information provided by pictures or other illustrations and information provided by the words in a text. **RI.7:** Use the illustrations and details in a text to describe its key ideas.

Use Visuals and Text

A visual can be a drawing, a picture, or a map. Visuals often give clues about the text. Text is something that is written. As you read, look at the visuals to help you understand the key ideas, or important information in the text.

Visuals help you understand what you will read.

Learn It

To help you use visuals and text:

1. **Before you read the text, look at the visuals. What do they show?**

2. **As you read the text, look for key ideas.**

3. **After you read, think about how the visuals and text help you understand the key ideas.**

Take out your bug spray and get ready for the swamps of southern United States! These swamps are near the Gulf Coast in Louisiana. Swamps are one kind of wetland. That means they are wet most, or all, of the year. A swamp is low land that is covered with water and plants.

The text gives key ideas.

U.S. Fish & Wildlife Service/Mark Musselman

What did you learn from the visual and text on page 54? Write down the key ideas below.

Key Ideas in Visuals

- trees
- _____
- _____

Key Ideas in Text

- These swamps are located in _____
- A wetland is _____
  _____
- A swamp is _____
  _____

McIntyre/PhotoLink/Getty Images

Read the text below and look at the picture. Underline key ideas.

Swamps are home to many kinds of animals. You would see everything from snakes and lizards to birds and fish. Of course, you can't forget about the alligators!

Word Study

 Common Core Standards
R.I.4: Ask and answer questions to help determine or clarify meaning of words and phrases in a text.

The list below shows some important words you will learn in this unit. Their definitions can be found on the next page. Read the words.

map

cardinal directions

globe

location

The Foldable on the next page will help you learn these important words. Follow the steps below to make your Foldable.

Step 1   Cut along the dotted blue lines.

Step 2   Fold along the dotted orange lines.

Trace the words and read their definitions.

Step 4   Complete the activities.

flickr RF/Getty Images

What place does this map show?

_____

A **map** is a drawing of a place.

Draw a (circle) around the picture that shows a globe.

A **globe** is a round model of Earth.

Cardinal directions are the directions of north, east, south, and west.

N stands for north. *E* stands for east. *S* stands for south. *W* stands for west.

Draw a (circle) around north.

A **location** is a place on Earth.

Ohio is a location, or place, on Earth. Can you name another location? Write it below.

_____

_____

57

globe

map

Fold Here

Fold Here

location

directions

cardinal

Primary Sources

A **letter** is one kind of primary source. You can learn a lot by reading letters. Letters can teach us about a time and a place from long ago. They can tell us about people's lives and important events in history.

Read the letter on the right. What do you learn about John's life?

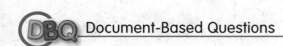 Document-Based Questions

1. **What does this letter describe?**

_____

2. **How can you tell this letter is from long ago?**

_____

_____

_____

My Dearest Beth,

We finally made it to California! The trip was long and hard. Often, the roads were so wet and muddy that the horses would not move. Can you imagine old Lilly pulling a muddy wagon? I miss you and our son.

Yours truly,

John

networks
connected.mcgraw-hill.com
● Skill Builders
● Resource Library

Map Elements

What do maps show?
What do you think?

_____

_____

_____

Word Hunt

Find and circle these words:

map   cardinal directions
symbol   compass rose
map key   *element

A compass rose shows the four cardinal directions: north, south, east, and west. The letter **N** stands for north. **S** stands for south. **W** stands for west and **E** stands for east.

Using Maps

Mrs. Stein's first grade class is learning about **maps**. A map is a drawing of a place. Mrs. Stein tells the class that maps show where places are located.

Neighborhood Map

FIRE STATION

POST OFFICE

Central Street

Orange Road

Lake Road

N
W E
S

Beach Drive

Maps show how to get from one place to another. Look at the map. It shows Mrs. Stein's neighborhood. It has some important **elements**, or parts, of a map.

> The title tells what the map shows.

Find the elements below on the map. Check the boxes after you find each element.

- [ ] title
- [ ] compass rose
- [ ] cardinal directions
- [ ] map key and symbols

Park Way

Map Key

School

Post Offiice

Fire Station

Homes

Golf Course

Beach

> Maps use **symbols**, or pictures and drawings, that stand for real things.

> A **map key** is a list of shapes and symbols used on a map. A map key is also called a map legend.

61

A Classroom Map

Look at the map below. It shows Mrs. Stein's classroom. Point to the map key with your finger. Look at the symbols for the art center and the computer lab. Draw a picture of the art center and computer lab in one of the blank boxes on the map. Don't forget to include the symbols!

Fill in the cardinal directions on the compass rose with the letters *S, E,* and *W.* The letter *N* has been filled in for you.

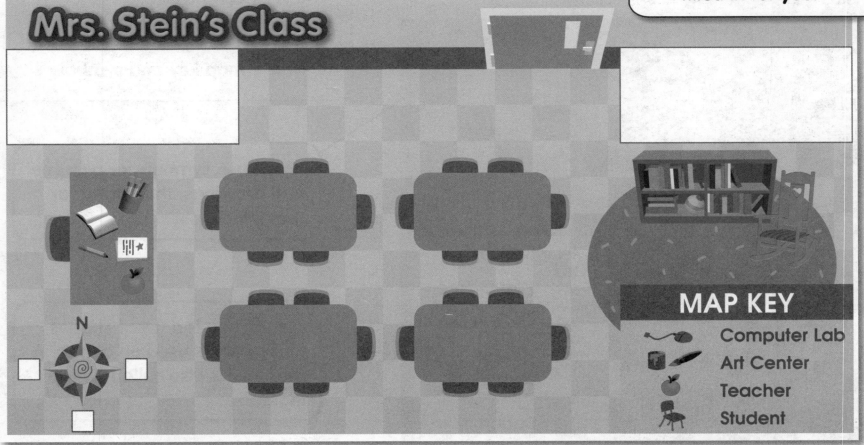

Mrs. Stein's Class

N

MAP KEY

Computer Lab

Art Center

Teacher

Student

Relative location and direction tells where something is by comparing it to another thing. Worlds like above, *below,* near, *far, and next to* tell the relative location of something.

_____

_____

_____

_____

Map and Globe Skills

(Circle) the title of the map on page 62. What does the map show?

_____

_____

_____

_____

Lesson 1

(?) **Essential Question** What do maps show?

_____

_____

_____

Go back to *Show As You Go!* on pages 52–53.

netw⊙rks **There's More Online!**
● Games ● Assessment

Maps and Globes

What can we learn from maps and globes?

What do you think?

_____

_____

_____

_____

Word Hunt

Find and (circle) these words:

political map   physical map

peninsula   globe

*model

Political Maps

Mrs. Stein asks the class if they have ever used a map before. Was it at the zoo, at the mall, or on a bus trip? "You are now going to learn about two different kinds of maps," says Mrs. Stein. "They are called political maps and physical maps. Let's begin with political maps!"

Leadner Baerenz/Digital Vision/Getty Images

"**Political maps** show borders, or lines, between areas. Borders show where a state or a country ends. This political map shows North Carolina and the states that border North Carolina," Mrs. Stein tells the class.

North Carolina Political Map

VIRGINIA

• Durham

Raleigh ★

NORTH CAROLINA

• Bynum

• Marion

SOUTH CAROLINA

Atlantic Ocean

GEORGIA

N
W   E
S

MAP KEY
★ Raleigh (capital)
• city
  my home

Ilene MacDonald/Alamy

DID YOU KNOW? The picture above shows an old state capitol building.

✏ Draw a picture of a house on the map. Then draw a symbol for the house on the map key.

Physical Maps

Now the class looks at a **physical map**. Mrs. Stein explains that physical maps show different kinds of land, such as peninsulas and swamps. Physical maps also show bodies of water, such as oceans, lakes, rivers, and gulfs. Look at the physical map. Do you live near any of the places on this map?

DID YOU KNOW?

Utah is home to The Bonneville Salt Flats. The smooth salt surface is ideal for auto and motorcycle racing.

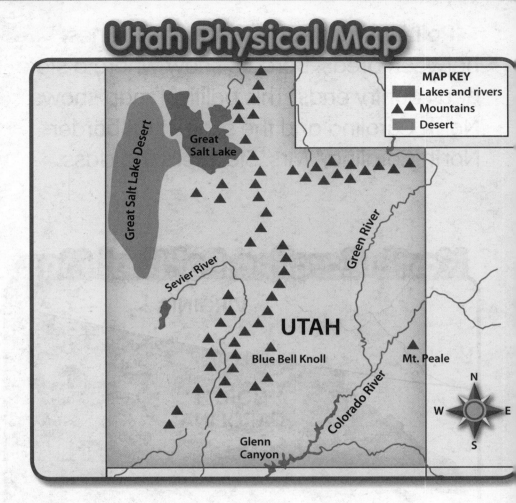

1. **Follow the Colorado River with your pencil.**

2. **Draw a circle around the Salt Lake Desert.**

Look at the pictures on the right. They show a place on the map. Write the letter for each place in the correct box on the map below.

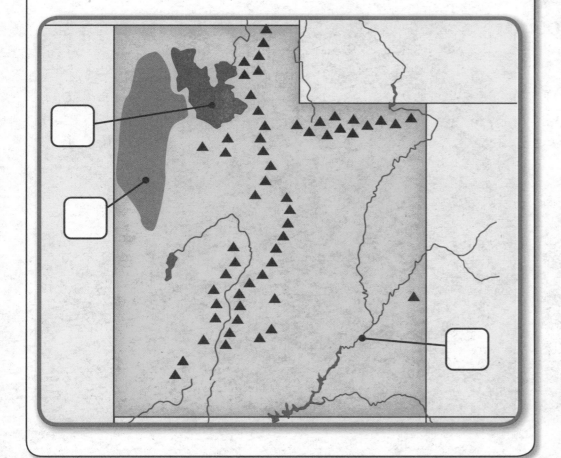

A. Great Salt Lake

B. Great Salt Lake Desert

C. Canyon along the Green River

Using Globes

Mrs. Stein's class is excited. Today, they are learning about **globes**. A globe is a round **model** of Earth.

Imagine you could look at Earth from space or like a bird. You would be able to see all the land and water on our planet! Globes show what Earth looks like from space. What parts are blue?

D. Hurst/Alamy Images

Some people today believe that people long ago thought our planet was flat. Tales have been told about sailors back then being afraid of falling off the edge of the Earth! But now we know that this is not true. Sailors have always known that the Earth is round.

Use the globe to complete the activities below.

1. **Draw a compass rose with the four cardinal directions.**

2. **Mark an ✕ on your state.**

3. **Draw a circle around the Atlantic Ocean and the Gulf of Mexico.**

Lesson **2**

? Essential Question What can we learn from maps and globes?

_____

_____

_____

Go back to *Show As You Go!* on pages 52–53

 **netw⊙rks** **There's More Online!**
● Games ● Assessment

Where We Live

? Essential Question

How does location affect our lives?

What do you think?

_____

_____

_____

_____

Word Hunt

Find and (circle) these words:

location   physical environment

transportation   weather

seasons   *affects

Around the World

People live in different places, or **locations**, on Earth. Some people live near water. Other people live near mountains or deserts. The land and water around us is called the **physical environment**.

Look at the pictures. Location **affects** people's needs, such as: homes, clothes, food, and transportation. **Transportation** is the way people move from place to place. Location also affects what we do for recreation, or fun.

Do you live near the ocean or a lake? Are you surrounded by land? Write about your physical environment on the lines below.

I live in _____

My physical environment includes _____

_____

Our World

Clothing

Work

ARCTIC OCEAN

NORTH
AMERICA
UNITED STATES

EUROPE

ASIA

ATLANTIC
OCEAN

AFRICA

PACIFIC
OCEAN

Equator

Equator

PACIFIC
OCEAN

SOUTH
AMERICA

INDIAN
OCEAN

AUSTRALIA

SOUTHERN
OCEAN

Recreation

ANTARCTICA

Food

Transportation

Shelter

Cloudy with a chance of...?

Did you check the **weather** today? Weather is how hot, cold, wet, or dry it is outside. Weather can change each day. One day it can be warm and sunny. The next day it can be cold and rainy.

Weather is different from place to place. Some places on Earth are cold all year while others are hot. Some places get little or no rain. Others get rainy weather or snow many days out of the year.

THINK · PAIR · SHARE
What is your favorite kind of weather? What is your least favorite?

What is the weather like today? Draw a picture to show how you will dress for the weather and what you will do for fun.

Seasons Change

In most places on Earth, the weather changes with the **seasons**. The seasons are the four parts of the year. They are spring, summer, fall, and winter.

Look at the pictures. Notice how the boys and girls are dressed and what they do for fun during each season.

FUN FACTS
The hottest day in the United States reached 134°F in Death Valley, California on July 10, 1913. The coldest day was -80°F in Alaska on January 23, 1971.

Write the name of each season in the boxes below.

Draw pictures below to show how location affects the way you live.

Homes

Transportation

Recreation

Food

Clothes

Lesson **3**

? Essential Question How does location affect our lives?

_____

_____

Go back to *Show As You Go!* on pages 52–53.

netwrks There's More Online!
⦿ Games ⦿ Assessment

2 Wrap Up

Read the riddles. Then find the word in the Word Bank that goes with each riddle.

Word Bank

compass rose

globe

peninsula

map key

political map

physical map

I can show all the land and water.
I am a round model of Earth.

_____

I am land with water on all sides but one.

_____

I can tell you which direction is north, south, east, and west.

_____

I show all the bumpy, lumpy parts of Earth. I can also show you where you will find the bodies of water.

_____

I show borders, or lines, between areas. You can use me to see where a state or a country ends.

_____

Some people call me a map legend.
I show shapes and symbols on a map.

_____

D. Hurst/Alamy Images

Big Idea Project

You are going to create a community map. Be sure to include your home, school, roads, and other places.

As you work, check off each task as you complete it.

My map...   **Yes it does!**

1. uses labels for places in my community.   ○

2. includes a title, a compass rose, and a map key with symbols.   ○

3. shows roads and route to school.   ○

4. is colorful and interesting.   ○

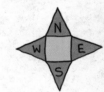

MAP KEY
HOME 🏠
PARK 🌴
SCHOOL 🏫
ROAD

● ●

Think About the Big Idea

BIG IDEA 💡 Location affects how people live. In your own words, explain the Big Idea on the lines below.

_____

_____

UNIT 3 Beginning Economics

You already know what it means to make choices. But do you know what we call making choices about money? The study of making choices about money is called economics. In this unit, you will learn all about economics and how it affects the choices you make.

Show As You Go!

After you read each lesson in this unit, use the pictures and the activities to practice what you are learning!

Lesson 1

After you read Lesson 1:

- (Circle) two goods in red.
- (Circle) two services in blue.

BANK Gifts PIZZA

Lesson 2

After you read Lesson 2:

- ◯ Draw an ↓ over someone spending money.

- ◯ Draw an ✕ over two people bartering.

Lesson 3

After you read Lesson 3:

- ◯ Draw your own store in the empty space below. Then draw a buyer and a seller exchanging goods in your store.

- ◯ Put a [box] around a producer.

Lesson 4

After you read Lesson 4:

- ◯ Describe what the people in the bank are doing.

  _____

  _____

- ◯ What is scarce in the picture below?

  _____

SURF SHOP

Diner

Hair Cuts

Juice

GRAPE SOLD OUT

Common Core Standards
RI2: Identify the main topic and retell key details of a text.

Main Topic and Details

Every story that you read has a main topic. The main topic tells what the story is about. Every story also has details. Details give more information. Finding the main topic and details will help you understand what you read.

Learn It

To find the main topic and details:

1. Read the story below.

2. Decide what the story is about. This is the main topic.

3. Look for details. They tell you more about the main topic.

My family and I had fun on our trip to the planetarium. We saw big models of planets there. We even met a scientist! I bought a toy rocket to take home with me. I liked our trip to the planetarium.

> This is the main topic.

> This is a detail. Find two more details in the story and <u>underline</u> them.

Paul S. Howell/Getty Images

Write the main topic and details from the story on page 80 in the chart below.

Main Topic

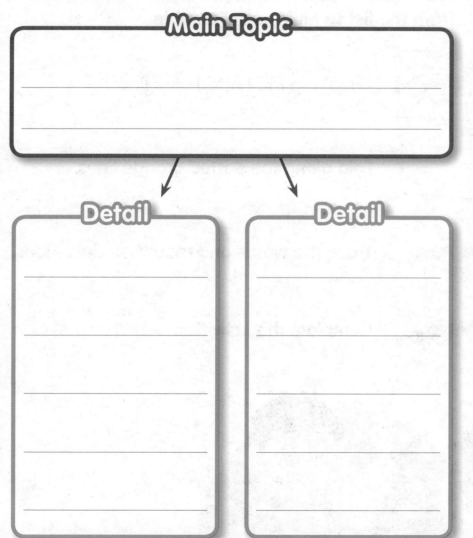

Detail

Detail

Read the story below. Circle the main topic. Underline the details.

On our trip we went to Myrtle Beach. We swam in the warm Atlantic Ocean. We made a big sand castle. We also went for a long walk and looked for seashells in the sand. I hope we go back to the beach soon!

Words to Know

Common Core Standards
RI4: Ask and answer questions to help determine or clarify the meaning of words and phrases in a text.

The list below shows some important words you will learn in this unit. Their definitions can be found on the next page. Read the words.

goods

services

barter

producers

buyers

scarce

FOLDABLES®

The Foldable on the next page will help you learn these important words. Follow the steps below to make your Foldable. After you finish these steps, use the words from the list to fill in your Foldable.

Step 1  Cut along the dotted blue lines.

Step 2  Fold along the dotted orange lines.

Step 3 Trace the words and read their definitions.

Step 4 Complete the activities.

John and Tom bartered. John gave Tom a baseball. **Tom gave John a**

_____ .

Circle the goods below.
- broom
- cheese
- student
- teacher
- pear
- TV

Draw a service worker below.

Barter means to give something and to get something else in return.

Goods are things people grow or make to sell.

A **service** is work done to help others.

Scarcity is when there is not enough of something.

A **buyer** is a person who buys goods.

A **producer** is a person who makes or grows goods to sell.

Jill does not have enough money. **What is scarce for Jill?**

_____

_____

Write a sentence about a time when you were a buyer.

_____

_____

Circle the producer.

scarce

buyer

producer

Fold Here

Fold Here

barter

goods

service

Primary Sources

Pictures are one type of primary source. A picture can be a photograph or a drawing. Pictures from long ago can show us what life was like in the past. We can learn about how people lived and what kind of jobs they did long ago. Look at this photograph. It is from the past. How can you tell that the photograph is from long ago?

DBQ Document-Based Questions

What does the picture on this page show?

_____

_____

What other kinds of work might people do?

_____

_____

networks
There's More Online!
● Resource Library
● Skill Builders

Lesson 1
Goods and Services

Essential Question

Why are goods and services important?

What do you think?

_____

_____

_____

_____

Word Hunt

Find and circle these words:

goods   services

*provide

Find 2 more new words:

_____

_____

What are goods?

Goods are things people make or grow to sell. Toys and clothes are goods that are made. Corn, strawberries, and beans are goods that are grown. Look around your classroom. What goods do you see?

What do you know about goods?

_____

_____

(tl)Iconotec/Alamy, (bl)Jamana images inc./Alamy(Royalty Free), (br)Ingram Publishing/Fotosearch

People make or grow goods to sell.
What are some things your family makes or grows?
What things do you have in your house that someone
made or grew for you?

Draw or glue pictures of goods below. Label your pictures.

What are services?

A **service** is work done to help others. Service jobs help meet people's needs and wants.

School workers, such as custodians, are service workers. They are paid for the services they do. They sweep the floors and clean the tables. Firefighters and police officers are also service workers. They risk their lives to keep us safe.

Draw or glue pictures of service workers below. Label your pictures.

What service do these firefighters provide?

_____

_____

Some businesses, like gas stations, **provide** both goods and services. A gas station sells goods like gas, oil, and maps. The station also provides a service when it sells its goods.

List other goods and services a gas station might provide. _____

_____

Think of another business that provides both goods and services. Then fill in the chart with the goods and services it provides.

Name of Business: _____

Goods	Services

Lesson 1

? **Essential Question** Why are goods and services important?

_____

_____

_____

Go back to *Show As You Go!* on pages 78–79. «

networks **There's More Online!**
● Games ● Assessment

Barter and Money

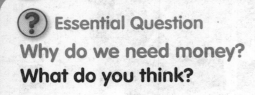

? **Essential Question**

Why do we need money?

What do you think?

_____

_____

_____

_____

Word Hunt

Find and (circle) these words:

barter money

*exchange

Find 2 more new words:

_____

_____

Barter, Barter, Barter

Long ago, people would **barter**, or trade, for things they needed or wanted. To barter means to give something and get something else in return.

What are the people in this picture bartering with?

_____

People would use things like beads, shells, or gold to barter. Through bartering, people got things that they would not have had otherwise.

THINK · PAIR · SHARE

Think of a time you traded something with someone. Was the trade fair? Why or why not?

Draw what you had that you traded.

Draw what you got in the trade.

Money, Money, Money

Ana and Sally have **money**. Money is something we use, or **exchange**, to buy goods and services. Money can be paper bills or coins.

Draw what Ana and Sally did to earn their money.

Ana and Sally want to go shopping with their money. Where can they buy a doll?

_____

_____

What two goods are Ana and Sally looking at?

_____

_____

Which one costs less money? Circle it!

$15.00 $10.00

What are Ana and Sally doing?

_____

_____

What is the man doing?

_____

_____

At last! Ana and Sally can enjoy their new doll!

Sequence Place the images below in the order they should happen. Put a number 1, 2, or 3 next to each picture.

Barter and Money

People still barter today. You might barter with your friends for goods and services. For example, you might exchange a blue bracelet for a purple one your friend has.

Today, most people use money because it is easy to carry around. Use the pictures to the right to complete the activity below.

Place a (circle) around the things that are easy to carry around.

Place a [box] around the things that are hard to carry around.

How are bartering and using money the same?

_____

_____

How are they different?

_____

_____

(t)Comstock Images/Getty Images, (c)Brand X Pictures/PunchStock, (cr)PhotoDisc/Getty Images, (b)GK Hart/ Vikki Hart/Stone/Getty Images

Design your own money! Draw a picture of what your money would look like.

Lesson ②

? **Essential Question** Why do we need money?

_____

_____

_____

Go back to *Show As You Go!* on pages 78–79.

netw⊙rks **There's More Online!**
● Games ● Assessment

Producers, Sellers, and Buyers

? Essential Question

Why do we need producers, sellers, and buyers?

What do you think?

_____

_____

_____

_____

Word Hunt

Find and circle these words:

producers   sellers

buyers

Find 2 more new words:

_____

_____

How goods and services get to us

Have you ever made or grown a good or service? If so, you are a producer! People who make or grow goods or provide services are called **producers**.

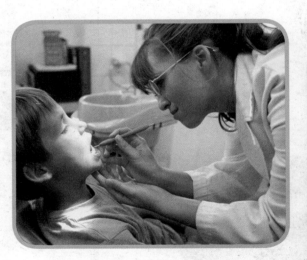

Providing a service

Producing a good

(l)Pixtal/AGE Fotostock, (r)Tanya Constantine/Photodisc/Getty Images

People who sell goods or services are known as **sellers**. Workers at a store who sell you a skateboard are sellers.

People use money to buy goods and services. That makes them **buyers**. You buy a skateboard with your money.

 Circle the buyer and place a box around the seller in the picture below.

Reading Skill

Main Topic and Details Fill in the chart below to show what you have learned about how we get goods and services.

Main Topic
how we get goods and services

Detail

Detail

Detail

97

Cause and Effect Fill in the missing text below by answering the question: How do buyers help producers?

Cause

Producers have goods to sell.

↓

Effect

Working Together

Producers, sellers, and buyers all work together to meet people's needs and wants. Producers make or grow goods to sell to buyers. Then they use the money they earn to buy more goods or services.

The pictures below are out of order. Label each photo with a number 1, 2, 3, or 4 to show the correct order.

Draw an example of a producer, a seller, or a buyer. Explain what your image shows on the lines.

_____

_____

_____

Is this boy a producer, seller, or buyer?

_____

Lesson 3

 Essential Question Why do we need producers, sellers, and buyers?

_____

_____

Go back to *Show As You Go!* on pages 78–79.

 **netw⊙rks** connected.mcgraw-hill.com
● Games ● Assessment

Making Choices

? Essential Question

Why do we make choices?

What do you think?

_____

_____

_____

_____

Word Hunt

Find and circle these words:

*choice   scarce

spend   save

opportunity cost

Find 2 more new words:

_____

_____

Scarcity and Choice

Imagine you want to play soccer and softball. But they are both played on the same day, at the same time. You have to make a **choice**.

 Draw a box around the activity you would choose below.

People do not have the time or money for everything they want. People have to choose what they will do and what they will buy.

People also have to make choices when their resources are **scarce**. When there is not enough of something, we say that it is scarce. Time, money, goods, or services are all resources. Scarcity leads to people having to make more choices.

People may choose to pay more for a scarce item, or they can shop somewhere else. Some people may decide to buy something different or nothing at all.

Look at the picture on the right. Milk is scarce for this man. He needs to make a choice. He can choose to go to the store to buy more milk. He can choose to eat his cereal without milk, or he can eat something else for breakfast.

Royalty-Free/Corbis

THINK · PAIR · SHARE
What do you think the man should do?

What resource is scarce for this man?

_____

_____

What to choose?

Remember, we have to make choices about time, money, and goods. David makes choices about how to **spend** his money. When he spends his money, he uses it to buy something.

First, David should spend his money on the things he needs, like pencils for school. Then, David can use the rest of his money to buy the things he wants. David wants a new baseball hat.

David may choose to **save** his money instead of buying a baseball hat. To save means to keep your money to spend later. David could save his money in his piggy bank over time. Then he would be able to buy something that costs more!

Match the word with the picture.

save

want

need

Time can also be scarce. Imagine that you have a lot of homework to do. You also want to watch your favorite TV show. You will have to choose between doing your homework and watching TV.

You choose to do your homework. Your homework needs to be turned in to your teacher tomorrow. You have to give up watching TV. The thing people give up to do something else is called the **opportunity cost**.

Watching TV is your

___ ___ ___ ___ ___ ___ ___ ___

___ ___ ___ ___.

Lesson **4**

? **Essential Question** **Why do we make choices?**

_____

_____

_____

Go back to *Show As You Go!* on pages 78–79. «

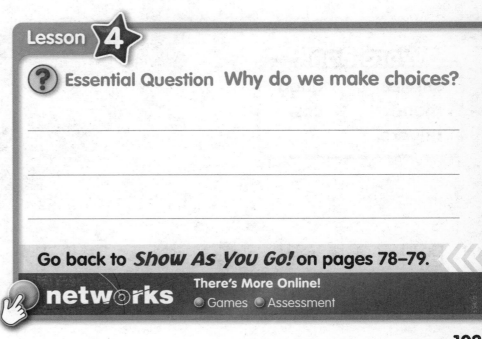

What do we study to learn about how people use money, goods, and services? To find the answer, fill in each blank inside the piggy bank. Then write the letters from the boxes on the numbered blank boxes below. Number 1 has been done for you.

Word Bank

service   good
money   cost
buyers

> People use ☐__☐____ to buy
> 6   4
> goods and services.

> A hamburger is an example of a ____☐__ .
> 3

> We use money to buy goods and services.
> That makes us ____ E ____ ____ ____ .
> 1

> If you buy a movie ticket instead of a book,
> the book is your opportunity ☐☐__ .
> 2   5

> Sweeping the floor is an example of a
> ☐ ____ ☐☐ .
> 9   7   8

E								
1	2	3	4	5	6	7	8	9

Big Idea Project

Welcome all producers! You are going to create a poster ad for a new good for your classroom store. Read the list below to see what you should include on your poster.

As you work, check off each task as you complete it.

My poster ad...   **Yes it does!**

1. has a picture of a good.   ○

2. includes a sentence describing the good.   ○

3. shows creativity and color.   ○

4. has a price under $10.   ○

Buy a new box of crayons for just $2.00!

Think About the Big Idea

BIG IDEA Economics affects choices. In your own words, explain the Big Idea on the lines below.

_____

_____

UNIT 4 Good Citizens

BIG IDEA People's actions affect others.

In this unit, you will learn about what it means to be a good citizen. There are many ways to be a good citizen! You can help others in your community. You can also follow rules at home, school, and in your community. As you read this unit, think about how your actions affect others and how you can be a good citizen.

networks™

connected.mcgraw-hill.com
- Skill Builders
- Vocabulary Flashcards

Show As You Go!

After you read each lesson in this unit, come back to these pages and complete these activities.

Lesson 1

After you read Lesson 1:

- Look for the pictures that show a rule. Write the word *rule* next to the pictures.

- Look for the pictures that show people following a law. Write the word *law* next to the pictures.

Lesson 2

After you read Lesson 2:
○ Draw a (circle) around the person using authority.

Lesson 3

After you read Lesson 3:
○ Put a [box] around people doing a service project.

Lesson 4

After you read Lesson 4:
○ Put a ☆ next to the symbols you see.

STOP

Lincoln Elementary School

No Littering

No Littering

Reading Skill

Common Core Standards
RI.8 Identify reasons an author gives to support points in a text.

Identify Author's Reasons

Authors, or writers, usually have a purpose for writing. They may want readers to think about something important or do something. Authors support these points by giving reasons.

As you read, think about whether the reasons support the author's point.

To help you identify an author's reasons:

1. **Read the story. Identify the author's main point.**

2. **Ask yourself:** *What does the author want me to think about or do?*

3. **Read the story again. Find the reasons that support the author's main point.**

It is important to pick up trash on our beaches. Trash makes our beaches look dirty and ugly. Trash can be dangerous. It can kill and harm our sea animals. Trash is also bad for the environment. Let's keep our beaches clean and safe!

> **This is the author's point.**

> **This is one reason that supports the author's main point. Underline two more reasons.**

Creatas/PunchStock

Write the author's point and reasons from the story on page 108 in the chart the below.

Author's Point

_____

_____

Reason

_____

_____

Reason

_____

_____

Reason

_____

_____

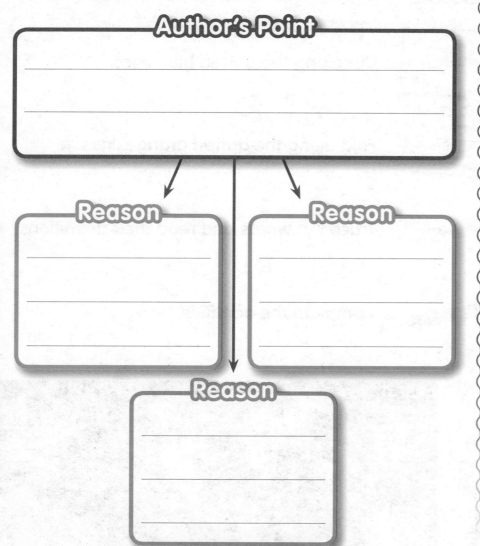

Read the story below. Circle the author's point. Underline three reasons.

Planting a garden is good for many reasons. It can help you relax. It is good exercise. But most of all, a garden will give you fresh fruits and vegetables. All this is good for your health!

Words to Know

FOLDABLES®

The list below shows some important words you will learn in this unit. Their definitions can be found on the next page. Read the words.

citizen

right

rule

law

conflict

symbol

The Foldable on the next page will help you learn these important words. Follow the steps below to make your Foldable.

Step 1  Cut along the dotted blue lines.

Step 2  Fold along the dotted orange lines.

Step 3 Trace the words and read their definitions.

Step 4 Complete the activities.

How can you be a good citizen in your classroom?

_____

_____

_____

Fold Here

Mark an X on the word that does not belong.

right   freedom

liberty   apple

What rule are the students following?

_____

A **citizen** is a person who belongs to a country.

A **right** is a freedom we have.

A **rule** tells us what we can and cannot do.

Do not fold

A **law** is a rule that everyone must follow.

A **conflict** is a problem between two or more people.

A **symbol** is something that stands for something else.

Fold Here

Write one more law below.
1. Drivers must stop at a red light.
2. Always wear seatbelts.
3.

Write about a conflict you have had at home or in school.

_____

_____

_____

The American flag is a symbol of our country. Draw a picture of the flag.

law

conflict

symbol

citizen

right

rule

Video and **audio recordings** are primary sources. A video recording is a picture with sound. Movies and TV shows are video recordings. An audio recording is a sound recording without video.

You can learn about people, places, and events by listening to and watching video and audio recordings. Look at the video on the right. It shows a news program about bullies in school.

 Document-Based Questions

1. **What is happening in the video?**

_____

2. **What advice would you give to the girl who is being bullied?**

_____

_____

_____

networks
There's More Online!
● Skill Builders
● Resource Library

We Are Citizens

? **Essential Question**

What does it mean to be a good citizen?

What do you think?

_____

_____

_____

_____

Word Hunt

Find and (circle) **these words:**

citizen	right
rule	responsibility
law	*belong

Find 2 more new words:

_____

_____

Good Citizens

It is Good Citizens Month at McKinley Elementary School! All month long, the students are going to be learning what it means to be good **citizens**. A citizen is a person who **belongs** to a country.

Good citizens follow rules and laws. They get along with others and help in their communities.

We are also citizens in our classrooms! There are many ways to be good citizens in our classroom and in our community. Read what these students have to say about being good citizens.

Gail Bulach/Concord Elementary School

"Good citizens show respect and kindness to people and animals. We talk and listen to each other when we have problems."

"Good citizens are responsible. We take care of our schools and communities. We help with classroom jobs."

"Good citizens make responsible decisions. We follow rules and laws so that something bad doesn't happen."

Reading Skill

Clarify Words and Phrases
Sometimes you may not understand the meaning of a word. When this happens, read the story again and look for clues. What do the words below mean?

Right:

_____

_____

_____

Responsibility:

_____

_____

_____

Rights and Responsibilities

Mrs. Garcia's students are learning about **rights** and **responsibilities**. A right is a freedom we have. We have the right to go to school and to be safe in school.

The students learn that a responsibility is a duty we have. We have the responsibility to come to school on time. It is also our responsibility to throw away litter, or trash, and to keep our schools and communities clean.

Leland Bobbe/Getty Images

Mrs. Garcia asked her students to put together a list of ways to be responsible citizens in school. Look at their list below.

Think of one more way to be responsible at school. Write it down next to the red star.

Responsible Citizens

★ Follow rules

★ Respect others

★ Arrive to school on time

★ Care about the environment

★

Draw a picture that shows one way to be a responsible citizen.

Rules at School

Today, Mrs. Garcia's class is learning about **rules**. "Rules tell us what we can and cannot do," she says. Mrs. Garcia reminds students that we follow rules at home, such as picking up after ourselves.

"We also follow rules in school. Rules keep order and help us to stay safe. One school rule is to wait our turn in line. This rule makes things fair for everyone," says Mrs. Garcia.

Underline the reasons we need rules in school.

Purestock/Getty Images

"We need rules in the classroom, too," says Mrs. Garcia. "One classroom rule is to raise our hands when we want to speak. This rule gives everyone in class a turn to speak and be heard."

"Can someone give me an example of another rule?" asks Mrs. Garcia. Julia raises her hand and says, "One rule is to respect each other and our belongings."

Mrs. Garcia needs one more rule. Can you think of a good rule for her class? Write it on the poster next to 4.

Mrs. Garcia's
Classroom Rules

1. Raise our hands to talk.

2. Be kind to each other.

3. Take turns.

4. _____

119

Laws in Our Community

The next day, Mrs. Garcia's class talks about **laws**. Mrs. Garcia explains that a law is a special kind of rule. "Our leaders make laws that everyone must follow. Like rules, laws also keep order and help us to stay safe."

Carlos raises his hand. He says, "My mom told me it is a law to follow street signs and lights."

"What happens if we do not follow this law?" asks Mrs. Garcia. "Everyone will get into accidents!" the students cry out.

Circle the pictures that show people following traffic laws.

Think of a new law for your community. Draw a picture of your law on the sign.

On the lines below, tell why you think this new law will help your community.

_____

_____

_____

_____

_____

Lesson **1**

 Essential Question What does it mean to be a good citizen?

_____

_____

_____

Go back to *Show As You Go!* on pages 106–107.

 **netw⊙rks** **There's More Online!**
● Games ● Assessment

People and Authority

(?) Essential Question

How can people's actions affect others?

What do you think?

_____

_____

_____

_____

Word Hunt

Find and (circle) these words:

authority   conflict

government   *decision

Find one more new word:

_____

People With Authority

This is Officer Sarah Duncan. She is going to talk to the students at McKinley Elementary about **authority**. The word _authority_ means power. People with authority make important **decisions**. They also help us follow rules and laws.

Mikael Karlsson

Fill in the boxes below with words, people, and ideas that help you understand the word _authority_. One example has been filled in.

```
┌──────────────────┐        ┌──────────────────┐
│                  │        │      power       │
└──────────────────┘        └──────────────────┘
            \                    /
             ( authority )
            /                    \
┌──────────────────┐        ┌──────────────────┐
│                  │        │                  │
└──────────────────┘        └──────────────────┘
```

Officer Sarah tells students that parents, teachers, and principals are people with authority. Teachers and principals keep order in school and make sure students are safe.

"Our **government** leaders also have authority," says Officer Sarah. "A government is a group of people who run a community, state, or country. Our government leaders help make laws."

Government affects the lives of individuals and families. The government requires citizens to pay taxes. These taxes provide services such as public education and health, roads, and security, like Officer Sarah.

Is Officer Sarah a person with authority? Explain.

_____

_____

_____

Comstock/ Getty Images

123

People Without Authority

"Sometimes people use power when they do not have authority," explains Officer Sarah. "They may steal something that does not belong to them."

"Some people force others to do things they do not want to do. This is called peer pressure. When you force someone to do something they do not want to do, you are being a bully."

"Using power without authority, can get people into trouble," says Officer Sarah.

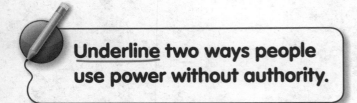

Underline two ways people use power without authority.

Read the story "Stop the Bully." Think about how Lola is using power without authority.

Stop the Bully
by Eric Johnson

Hey, Lisa. Wait up! What's for lunch?

Umm,...I'm having a turkey sandwich, carrots, and a cookie that my mom made for me.

1

Is something wrong, Lisa?

Oh, nothing. I just hurt my knee.

4

How do you think this story ends? Draw a picture.

Solving Conflicts

A **conflict** is a problem between two or more people. In the story you just read, the conflict is between Lola and Lisa. Lola is a bully. Her actions are hurting Lisa.

There are many ways to solve a conflict. Look at the poster below. It shows ways to solve conflicts.

How to Solve Conflicts

Talk
- Talk to the person you have a conflict with.
- Tell him or her what you feel is the problem.

Share
- Don't be afraid to share your feelings.

Listen
- Listen to the other person's thoughts and feelings.

Role play
- Ask someone to help you role play how to solve the conflict.

Sometimes, you may need to ask an adult to help you solve a conflict. In the story, Lisa talked to her teacher about the problems she was having. Teachers, principals, and parents can help solve conflicts.

THINK · PAIR · SHARE
Think about a conflict you have had. How did you solve it? Work with a buddy to talk about a conflict you had and how you solved it.

Lesson **2**

? **Essential Question** How do people's actions affect others?

_____

_____

_____

Go back to *Show As You Go!* on pages 106–107.

 **netw⊙rks** **There's More Online!**
● Games ● Assessment

Good Citizens Help

How can citizens make a difference?
What do you think?

_____

_____

_____

_____

Helping Our Schools and Communities

Each year, the students at McKinley Elementary take part in a school **service project**. A service project is a school or community **activity**. Service projects allow students to learn how to make decisions and help others at the same time.

What kind of service project is this boy doing?

_____

_____

_____

Ken Karp/McGraw-Hill Education

Word Hunt

Find and (circle) **these words:**

service project   *activity

Find 2 more new words:

_____

_____

Last year, the students helped to clean their school. They also picked up trash in their community and learned how to take care of the environment.

The poster below shows other projects students have worked on. Can you give the students an idea for next year's project? Write your idea next to the star.

 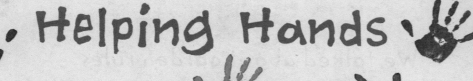 **Helping Hands**

* **Collect school supplies**

* **Cook meals for sick people**

* **Read or tutor children**

* **Plant school and community gardens**

* _____

A School Service Project

This year, students at McKinley Elementary helped to plant a school and community garden. This is a book Grace made about the project.

 (Circle) the page from Grace's book that tells about helping the community.

Grace's Service Project Book

Planting a Garden

Safety First

We talked about garden rules. Good citizens always follow rules.

★ ★ ★ Garden Rules ★ ★ ★

1. No running with tools.

2. Walk with tools by your side.

3. Return tools to their place.

4. No walking on plants.

Alistair Berg/Getty Images

Dig In!

We planted our garden!
We planted rows of carrots,
lettuce, peas, and potatoes.

Helping Others!

The veggies will go to
people who do not have
food. It is our way of
helping our community.

Water, Water, Water

One of our classroom jobs is
to water the garden. We all
take turns and watch our
garden grow.

(t)Lifesize/Getty Images, (tr)Image Source/Punchstock, (b)©Corbis Premium RF/Alamy

Lesson 3

 Essential Question How can citizens make a
difference?

_____

_____

_____

Go back to *Show As You Go!* on pages 106–107. «

 **networks** There's More Online!
● Games ● Assessment

Symbols of Our Country

? Essential Question

How do people and symbols stand for America?

What do you think?

_____

_____

_____

_____

Word Hunt

Find and (circle) these words:

symbol   democracy

*pledge

Find 2 more new words:

_____

_____

American Symbols

On the last week of Good Citizens Month, students at McKinley Elementary make a book about American **symbols**. A symbol is something that stands for something else. People, statues, and animals can be symbols. American symbols show we are proud of our country.

Image Source/Getty Images

Draw a star ☆ next to any symbols you know about.

The United States of America is a **democracy**. A democracy is a government that is run by its people. In a democracy, people make decisions that affect the country. They can choose their leaders and help make laws.

DID YOU KNOW?
We have symbols that stand for our country's democracy. The Statue of Liberty, the American flag, and the bald eagle are American symbols.

Purestock/PunchStock

133

Our Flag

by Roberto Díaz

The United States flag is a symbol of our country. Our flag stands for liberty and freedom. The colors on our flag are red, white, and blue. Our flag has 13 stripes and 50 stars. There is a star for each state.

We celebrate our country with the flag. We raise our flag on holidays. We wave it during parades. We say the Pledge of Allegiance to it. To pledge allegiance means to promise to be loyal.

Blend Images/PunchStock

The Pledge of Allegiance

I **pledge** allegiance to the flag
of the United States of America
and to the Republic for which it stands,
one Nation under God, indivisible,
with liberty and justice for all.

Color the United States flag.

Can you guess which song begins with the words, *Oh, say can you see…?* It is our national anthem, The Star-Spangled Banner! We sing the national anthem to honor our flag and the people who fought for our country. We stand during the song to show respect for our flag.

What does the Pledge of Allegiance mean to you? Write about it on the lines below.

_____

_____

_____

_____

The Statue of Liberty

by Melissa Ling

The Statue of Liberty is a symbol of freedom, hope, and friendship. The Statue of Liberty is in New York City.

Today, people from all over the world visit the Statue of Liberty. The statue stands for friendship because she welcomes everyone.

(t)Blend Images/PunchStock, (r)Image Source/Getty Images

Reading Skill

Ask and Answer Questions
As you read, think about the key details. Ask and answer questions to make sure you understand what you read.

Why does the Statue of Liberty stand for friendship?

_____

_____

_____

The Bald Eagle

by Aaron Jones, Jr.

When America became a free country, it needed a symbol. Our leaders wanted a symbol to stand for our country's democracy. They chose the bald eagle.

The bald eagle is big and strong. Our country is big and strong, too. The bald eagle stands for a strong, proud, and free America.

Reading Skill
Author's Reasons (Circle) the reasons why the bald eagle is a symbol.

(t)Blend Images/PunchStock, (b)Purestock/PunchStock

Our Presidents

by Gabby Miller

The President is the leader of our country. Like symbols, Presidents also stand for our country. They show leadership, courage, and responsibility.

George Washington and Abraham Lincoln are two of my favorite Presidents. They fought for freedom in the United States. How do our President today and past Presidents stand for America?

The Washington Monument honors George Washington.

The Lincoln Memorial honors Abraham Lincoln.

Guess the Symbol

Match the number of the clue below to its symbol above.

1. You can visit me in New York City. I welcome people from all over the world. I stand for freedom and hope.

2. I am red, white, and blue. You can call me by my nickname, "The Star-Spangled Banner." I stand for liberty.

3. I am big and strong. I soar through the sky. I stand for a strong, proud, and free America.

Purestock/PunchStock

Lesson 4

? **Essential Question** How do people and symbols stand for America?

_____

_____

_____

Go back to *Show As You Go!* on pages 106–107.

 **networks** There's More Online!
● Games ● Assessment

Read each definition to help you unscramble the words below.

1. **tuoratyih** _____ _____ _____ _____ _____ _____ _____ _____
   to have power

2. **itzecni** _____ _____ _____ _____ _____ _____ _____
   a person who belongs to a country

3. **htgir** _____ _____ _____ _____ _____
   a freedom we have

4. **ncfticol** _____ _____ _____ _____ _____ _____ _____ _____
   a problem between two or more people

5. **luer** _____ _____ _____ _____
   tells us what we can and cannot do

6. **yboslm** _____ _____ _____ _____ _____ _____
   something that stands for something else

(l)Ingram Publishing/age fotostock, (lc)Ken Cavanagh/McGraw-Hill Education, (lr)Ken Cavanagh/McGraw-Hill Education, (r)Ableod Images/PunchStock

Big Idea Project

Here is your chance to be an actor! You will create a "Good Citizens" skit that shows others how to be good citizens.

Read the list below to help you create your skit.

Our skit. . .   **Yes it does!**

1. shows how people can be good citizens at home, school, or in the community.   ◯

2. has a speaking part for each person in the group.   ◯

3. shows that we worked together as a team.   ◯

4. shows that we have practiced and are ready to perform for our class.   ◯

• •

Think About the Big Idea

BIG IDEA 💡 **People's actions affect others. In your own words, explain the Big Idea on the lines below.**

_____

_____

Picture Glossary

A

*activity   An activity is something we do for fun.

*affect   Affect means to make something happen.

authority   Authority means to have the power to make decisions.

B

barter   Barter means to give something and get something else in return.

buyers Buyers are people who use money to buy goods and services.

cardinal directions Cardinal directions are the directions of north, south, east, and west.

*celebration A celebration is a special way to honor a person, place, or event.

character Character means having or showing honesty, courage, or responsibility.

*choice A choice is something to pick from.

citizen A citizen is a person who belongs to a country.

(c)Ryan McVay/Getty Images, (b)eVStock/Alamy

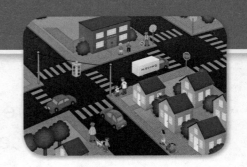

community   A community is a place where people live, work, and play.

compass rose   A compass rose shows the four cardinal directions.

conflict   A conflict is a problem between two or more people.

*courage   Courage means to do something without fear.

culture   Culture is the way a group of people live. It is made up of a group's special food, music, and art.

(b)Glow Images

D

*decision   A decision is a choice to be made.

democracy   A democracy is a government that is run by its people.

E

*element   An element is a part of something.

exaggerate   Exaggerate means to make something bigger or more important than it is.

*exchange   Exchange means to give up something for something else.

F

fable   A fable is a made-up story that teaches a lesson.

*fact   A fact is something that is true and not made up.

fiction   Fiction is something that is not true.

G

globe   A globe is a round model of Earth.

goods   Goods are things people buy or grow to sell.

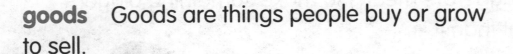

government   A government is a group of people who run a community, state, or country.

H

history   History is the story of people and events from other times and places.

(t)D. Hurst/Alamy, (tc)Mitch Hrdlicka/Getty Images, (b)Library of Congress - Prints and Photographs Division (LC-USZC4-6877)

holiday A holiday is a day when we remember and honor a special event or person. (p. 24)

*honesty Honesty means to be honest or truthful.

L

law A law is a rule that everyone must follow.

location A location is a place on Earth.

M

map A map is a drawing of a place.

(t)Tetra Images/Getty Images, (tc)Blend Images/Alamy Images, (bc)Royalty-Free/CORBIS

map key   A map key is a list of shapes and symbols used on a map. A map key is also called a map legend.

*model   A model is a small copy of something.

money   Money is something we use to buy goods and services.

N

nonfiction   Nonfiction tells about something true.

O

opportunity cost   Opportunity cost is what people give up to do or have something else.

P

peninsula A peninsula is land with water on all sides except one.

physical environment Physical environment is the land and bodies of water around us.

physical map Physical maps show land and bodies of water.

*pledge A pledge is a promise.

political map Political maps show borders, or lines, between areas.

(tc)courtesy of the State Archives of Florida, (bc)Digital Vision/PunchStock

producers   Producers are people who make or grow goods to sell.

*provide   Provide means to give.

responsibility   A responsibility is a duty we have. (pages 38 and 116)

right   A right is a freedom we have.

rule   A rule tells us what we can and cannot do.

save   To save means to keep your money in order to spend it later.

(t)Tanya Constantine/Photodisc/Getty Images, (tc)Image Source/Punchstock, (bc)Ingram Publishing

scarce   When there is not enough of something it is scarce.

season   A season is one of the four parts of the year.

seller   Sellers are people who sell goods and services.

service   A service is work done to help others.

slavery   Slavery means that one person takes away another person's freedom.

spend   Spend is to use money to buy something.

symbol   A symbol is something that stands for something else.

T

tall tale   A tall tale is a story that exaggerates details.

technology   Technology is the science of making things faster and easier.

(b)Creatas/PunchStock

time line   A time line is a line that shows an order of events.

transportation   Transportation is the way people move from place to place.

W

weather   Weather is how hot, cold, wet, or dry it is outside.

(b)blue jean images RF/Getty Images

Index

This index lists many topics you can find in your book. It tells the page numbers on which they are found. If you see the letter *m* before a page number, you will find a map on that page.